discover countries

The United Kingdom

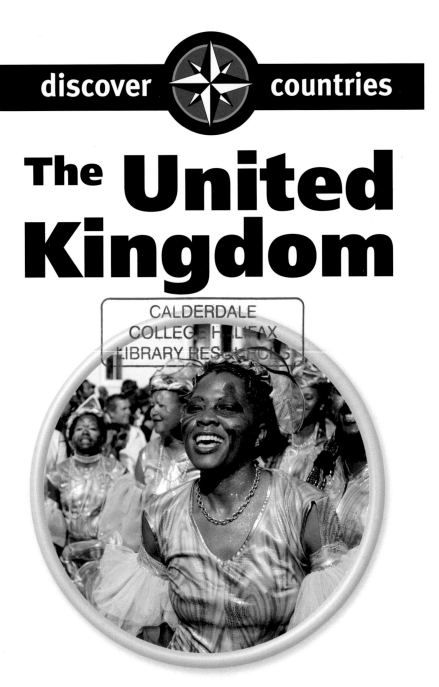

Tim Atkinson

WAYLAND

D0319280

First published in 2010 by Wayland
Copyright Wayland 2010
This paperback edition published in 2012

Wayland
Hachette Children's Books
338 Euston Road
London NW1 3BH

Wayland Australia
Level 17/207 Kent Street,
Sydney, NSW 2000

Concept design: Jason Billin
Editor: Susan Crean
Designer: Clare Nicholas
Consultants: Rob Bowden and Elaine Jackson, OFSTED inspector
and chair of the Geographical Association's Primary and Early Years Committee

Produced for Wayland by
White-Thomson Publishing Ltd

www.wtpub.co.uk
+44 (0)845 362 8240

British Library Cataloguing in Publication Data

Atkinson, Tim.
United Kingdom. – (Discover countries)
1. Great Britain–Juvenile literature.
I. Title II. Series
941'.086-dc22

ISBN: 978 0 7502 6783 0

Printed in China
Wayland is a division of Hachette Children's Books
an Hachette UK company
www.hachette.co.uk

All data in this book was updated in 2011
and has been collected from the latest sources available at that time.

Picture credits
1, Dreamstime/Patrick Wang; 3 Photoshot/Jon Arnold Travel (top), EASI-Images/Rob Bowden (bottom); 4 (map), Stefan Chabluk; 5, Photoshot/Jon Arnold Travel; 6, Dreamstime; 7, Dreamstime; 8, Dreamstime; 9, iStock/Chris Schmidt; 10, Shutterstock/Pres Panayotov; 11, Dreamstime/David Martyn; 12, Photolibrary/Rod Edwards; 13, EASI-Images/Rob Bowden; 14, Photolibrary/Superstock; 15, WTPix/Chris Fairclough; 16, Corbis/Andrew Fox; 17, iStock; 18, Photolibrary/Alan Chandler; 19, Getty Images/Gen Nishino; 20, Shutterstock/David Iliff; 21, Dreamstime/Stephen Meese; 22, Shutterstock; 23, SWT/Steve White Thomson (top) and iStock Photo/Joanne Green (bottom); 24, Dreamstime/David Martyn; 25 Photolibrary/Jon Arnold Travel; 26, Shutterstock/Kevin Eaves; 27, Dreamstime/Patrick Wang (top) and Shutterstock/Chris Green (bottom); 28, Photolibrary/Brian Lightfoot; 29, Corbis/Gideon Mendel (top) and Eye Ubiquitous/Hutchison (bottom) Front cover images, Photoshot/Jon Arnold Travel (left), Dreamstime (right)

Contents

Discovering the United Kingdom

The United Kingdom (UK) is located 34 kilometres (21 miles) off the coast of mainland Europe. Once the vast British Empire spanned the globe, and today the UK is a mix of peoples and cultures from around the world.

A land of islands

The UK is a political union of four separate nations in the British Isles. Three of them – England, Scotland and Wales – occupy the same island which is known as Great Britain. The fourth nation – Northern Ireland – makes up part of the other major island in the British Isles. The Republic of Ireland, which takes up the southern part of the same island, is the only country that borders the UK. The UK also includes more than 1,000 smaller offshore islands.

The British Empire

In the past, Great Britain ruled an empire which covered almost one-quarter of the Earth's land. Today the UK and many of the countries that used to be part of the British Empire are members of the Commonwealth of Nations.

Key
- ■ Capital city
- ■ Provincial capital city
- ● Other cities
- △ Mountain

0 100 miles
0 100 kilometres

Orkney Islands

North Atlantic Ocean

Shetland Islands

SCOTTISH HIGHLANDS

△ Ben Nevis

SCOTLAND

Glasgow Edinburgh

North Sea

N
W   E
S

NORTHERN IRELAND

Belfast

Isle of Man

LAKE DISTRICT

U N I T E D

IRELAND

Irish Sea

K I N G D O M

Manchester

● Sheffield

ENGLAND

Leicester

Birmingham

WALES

Cardiff

River Thames

London

English Channel

Isles of Scilly

Channel Islands

FRANCE

 The Houses of Parliament in London are the home of the UK government. The clock-tower is known as Big Ben.

Besides the UK, the biggest countries in the Commonwealth are Canada, Australia, New Zealand and Jamaica. The Queen is the Head of State for these and all 16 countries that make up the Commonwealth. About 30 per cent of the world's population lives in a Commonwealth country.

The UK today

The Head of State in the UK is the monarch (at present, Queen Elizabeth II). The UK's government is elected by the people. It is based in London. It is led by a prime minister who is the leader of the largest political party in the UK Parliament. There are also governments for Scotland, Wales and Northern Ireland. They are each based in a capital city, too (Edinburgh, Cardiff and Belfast).

The UK economy is the fifth-largest economy in the world and the second-largest in Europe (after Germany). London is one of the two biggest financial centres in the world, the other being New York City in the USA.

United Kingdom Statistics

Area: 244,820 sq km (94,526 sq miles)

Capital city: London

Government type: Constitutional Monarchy

Bordering countries: Republic of Ireland

Currency: Sterling £ (GBP)

Language: English, Welsh (26% of Wales), Scottish Gaelic (1.2% of Scotland); Irish Gaelic (5% of Northern Ireland)

Landscape and climate

The United Kingdom is mostly surrounded by the sea, and nowhere in the UK is more than 113 km (70 miles) from the coast. The country's landscapes vary from high mountain ranges to low, flat plains.

The seaside

With so much coastline, the seaside forms much of the UK landscape. Some of the UK's most famous coastal landscapes include the White Cliffs of Dover in south-east England and the Giant's Causeway in Northern Ireland. This dramatic sight is made up of 40,000 rock columns rising up from the sea.

Another of the UK's most important seaside landscapes is the Jurassic Coast, in the south-west of England. Its landscapes show the long history of the land. By looking at the cliffs along a stretch of coastline, people can see rocks dating back billions of years.

A varied landscape

Away from the coast, the UK's landscape is different in each of its regions. The Highlands of Scotland, the Cambrian Mountains in Wales and the Lake District in northern England contain the country's highest mountains. Ben Nevis in Scotland is the UK's highest mountain.

DID YOU KNOW?

The UK's coastline is 12,429 kilometres (7,723 miles) long. That's as far as it is from Beijing in China to Paris, France!

The Dorset and East Devon coastline is also known as the Jurassic Coast. It is one of two natural World Heritage Sites in the UK's main islands. The other is the Giant's Causeway in Northern Ireland.

Facts at a glance

Land area: 241,590 sq km (93,278 sq miles)

Water area: 3,230 sq km (1,250 sq miles)

Highest point: Ben Nevis 1,343 m (4,406 ft)

Lowest point: The Fens –4 m (–13.1 ft)

Longest river: River Severn 290 km (180 miles)

Coastline: 12,429km (7,723 miles)

There are chalk hills in central and southern England, while parts of eastern England contain large areas of wide, flat land that were once wetlands. The water was drained from this region to gain more land for farming. Some of these areas are actually several metres below sea-level. This land is very good for farming.

British weather

The climate in the UK is temperate and seasonal. The main influence on the British weather is a warm ocean current called the Gulf Stream. It flows from the Gulf of Mexico northwards across the Atlantic Ocean, carrying warm waters with it. The Gulf Stream keeps the UK warmer than other countries on the same latitude. Moisture from the air warmed by the Gulf Stream also makes parts of the UK among the wettest places in Europe.

The Scottish Highlands have an average of 4,000 mm (158 inches) of rain each year. The driest parts of England get just 500 mm (20 inches) of rain each year. Although the weather varies from region to region and from season to season, the UK does not usually suffer any extremes of weather such as hurricanes.

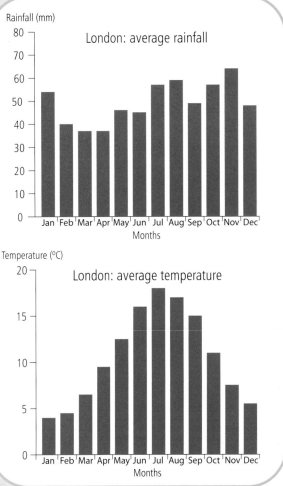

▼ Snow is a common feature of winters in Scotland, which contains some of the UK's least-populated areas.

Population and health

People in the UK enjoy all the benefits of living in a modern, industrial society. Most people live healthy and long lives and are able to work. These qualities make the UK attractive to people from other countries, and many immigrants have come to live in the UK.

An ageing population

There are more old-age pensioners in the UK than people under the age of 16. This is because people have fewer children than they once did. People in the UK are also living longer today than in the past.

Facts at a glance

Total population: 62 million

Life expectancy at birth: 80.05 years

Children dying before the age of five: 0.6 %

Ethnic composition: white 92.1% (of which English 83.6%, Scottish 8.6%, Welsh 4.9%, Northern Irish 2.9%), black 2%, Indian 1.8%, Pakistani 1.3%, mixed 1.2%, other 1.6% (2001 census)

▼ Some older people in the UK keep fit by playing bowls.

Immigration

The falling birth rate has led to a shortage of workers in some areas. To fill these vacancies, people from other European Union countries have been coming to the UK in recent years. For example, more than 96,000 people from Poland came to live and work in the UK in 2007. However, the Irish Republic is the EU country with the largest number of workers living in the UK. About half a million people born in the Republic of Ireland live in Britain.

People have been migrating to the UK for centuries. Many moved to the UK because their home country was once part of the British Empire. Since the 1950s, millions of people from former British colonies have moved to the UK. So people of Australian, Indian, Pakistani, West Indian and Bangladeshi origin make up part of the UK population.

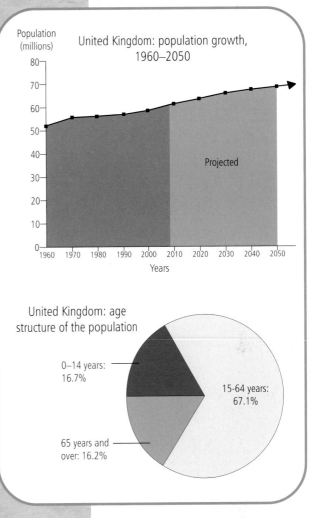

United Kingdom: population growth, 1960–2050

Population (millions)

Projected

Years

United Kingdom: age structure of the population

0–14 years: 16.7%

15-64 years: 67.1%

65 years and over: 16.2%

The National Health Service

Since 1948 people in the UK have had access to free health care through the National Health Service (NHS). This ensures everyone can get the medical care they need, regardless of wealth. One thing the NHS has been trying to do in recent years is reduce the number of premature deaths due to heart disease. Heart disease is the biggest killer in the UK.

DID YOU KNOW?

In 1948 the NHS cost £280 million to run. The figure now stands at over £105 billion – more than 375 times more than when the NHS was first created!

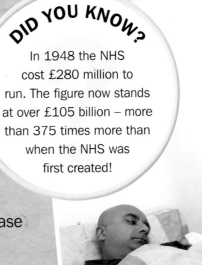

▶ NHS nurses have a wide range of responsibilities. Nurses form the largest group of staff in the NHS.

Settlements and living

More than 80 per cent of people in the UK live in towns or cities. The UK's three largest cities – London, Birmingham and Manchester – together provide a home to almost 13 million people, which is more than 20 per cent of the UK population.

Nation of homeowners

More than 75 per cent of people in the UK own the house or flat in which they live rather than renting. This gives the UK one of the highest rates of owner-occupation in the world. But the price of houses in the UK is high, and many young people find it very difficult to afford a suitable home. The UK government has promised that it will make sure enough new homes are built each year to ease this problem.

Moving up

In the 1960s many high-rise flats were built in order to prevent a housing shortage. A number of these estates have since suffered badly from social problems such as vandalism, and they often have high crime rates.

Facts at a glance

Urban population: 89.7% (54.1 million)

Rural population: 10.3% (6.2 million)

Population of largest city: 8.6 million (London)

▼ In urban areas such as London, large Victorian houses are often made into flats. The high-rise buildings in the background show a more modern solution to housing shortages.

Local authorities have demolished the worst estates, such as Hulme in Manchester and Norfolk Park in Sheffield. In their place they have built traditional flats and houses.

The countryside

For centuries, the countries of the UK had many rural settlements. Villages can still be found dotted throughout the UK countryside today. In many places, laws restrict the building of new homes in rural areas. There is a lot of pressure, however, for the government to allow people to build new homes in these places to help ensure that enough new homes are being built each year for the expanding population.

▶ In the English countryside people often have more space and houses can be larger than in city centres.

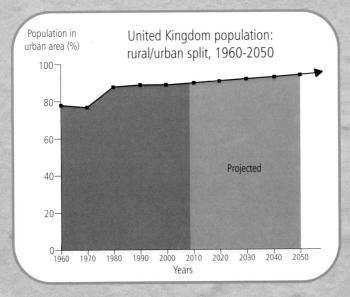

Population in urban area (%)

United Kingdom population: rural/urban split, 1960-2050

Projected

Years

DID YOU KNOW?
Over 400,000 people in the UK live in national parks. In Scotland and England, 12 national parks take up about 8.5 per cent of the total land area. In Wales, three national parks cover 20 per cent of the land area!

Family life

Family life has traditionally been important to people in the United Kingdom. However, people are choosing to have fewer children than in the past. As a result, family units are becoming smaller.

A changing focus

In recent years, there has been a rise in the number of single-person households. In 2007 the number of people living alone, rather than as part of a family, was double what it had been in 1971. Overall, people in the UK now think that having close friends is more important than keeping strong ties with their family.

Working and living

Many British children's parents both work outside the home. The British government tries to encourage parents to return to work after having children. It does this by helping to pay some of the cost of nursery schools.

The UK has a high teenage pregnancy rate compared to other EU countries. However, most women who have children do so later, around the age of 30.

Facts at a glance

Average children per childbearing woman:
1.9 children

Average household size:
2.4 people

▼ A family relaxes with a picnic outside a motorhome in Pembrokeshire, Wales. Camping and caravanning are popular ways for families to spend time together in the UK.

Getting married

There are three forms of partnership in the UK – marriage, cohabitation (living together) and civil partnerships. Of these, marriage is the most common form of partnership in the UK, although the number of people getting married is falling. In 2006 there were 236,980 marriages in England and Wales, which is the lowest number of marriages since 1895. This is because more people in the UK are choosing to live together without getting married.

Family history

Family life is not as important as it used to be in the UK. However, 60 per cent of people in the UK spend time each year researching their family tree. The Internet has made it much easier for people to find out about their ancestors, and there are now hundreds of websites where people can search for their relatives. The breakdown of the traditional family unit seems to have created a need for people to find out as much as they can about their ancestors.

DID YOU KNOW?
The British are regarded as a nation of dog-lovers. Nearly 20 per cent of UK households have a dog, while 52 per cent of UK families own some sort of pet.

⬆ In the UK today, an average wedding celebration costs more than £20,000. However, getting married itself is not expensive. Couples can get married for about £100.

Religion and beliefs

More than two-thirds of the people in the UK are Christian, although the number of people going to church is small. Nearly 60 per cent of the population never goes to church at all. Other religions have grown as people from abroad have settled in the UK. Today there are many Muslims, Hindus, Jews and Sikhs.

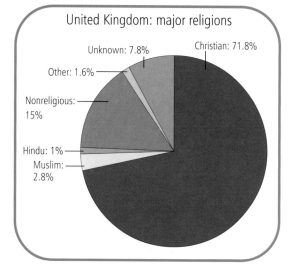

United Kingdom: major religions

Christian: 71.8%
Unknown: 7.8%
Other: 1.6%
Nonreligious: 15%
Hindu: 1%
Muslim: 2.8%

Open to religion

The people of the UK are welcoming of different religions. Today, the UK has the second-largest Jewish population in Europe. About half the 300,000 British Jews live in London, with the rest living mainly in urban areas. The largest Muslim groups came from Pakistan and Bangladesh. The UK also has more than 150,000 Buddhists.

The Christian Church

Christianity is the main religion in the UK. Anglicans, as members of the Church of England are known, make up the largest group of Christians in the UK. The Head of the Church of England is the Queen.

The number of Roman Catholics in the UK is growing as people from Poland and other European Countries with a large number of Catholics come to live in Britain.

▼ Canterbury Cathedral is the UK's most important Christian church. There has been a cathedral in Canterbury for almost 1,500 years.

Religious festivals

People in the UK celebrate festivals related to their religion. For example, Christians celebrate Christmas across the UK by giving and receiving Christmas presents and eating a large Christmas Day lunch. Christians in the UK traditionally give up something such as sweets during Lent, which is the 40 days leading up to the important Christian festival of Easter.

Muslims mark the holy month of Ramadan by going without food between sunrise and sunset. And for Hindus and Sikhs living in Britain, Diwali – the Festival of Lights – is celebrated by lighting lamps and holding firework displays. These are especially impressive in the British city of Leicester, which has a large Asian population.

🔺 Diwali and Annakut are the biggest festivals celebrated every year at the Hindu temple in Neasden, London. During Annakut, or the Hindu New Year, more than 1,000 vegetarian foods are laid out inside the temple as an offering to Hindu gods and goddesses.

DID YOU KNOW? The largest Hindu temple outside India is in Neasden, London. Over 4,000 tonnes of stone were used to build the temple, which was completed in 1995. The temple cost £12 million to build.

Education and learning

Children in the UK must start school by the age of five (or four in Northern Ireland). They begin by going to a primary school. At the age of 11 they move to secondary school, and they remain at school until they are at least 16. The school leaving age is being raised in the UK, and by 2013 students will be required to stay in full-time education until the age of 18.

Facts at a glance

Children in primary school:
Male 99%, Female 99%

Children in secondary school:
Male 94%, Female 97%

Literacy rate (over 15 years):
99%

Learning and work

At the age of 14, students in the UK are expected to focus their studies on specific subjects. In addition to traditional examinations (such as GCSEs and A Levels) a variety of diplomas are now available in subjects such as engineering, manufacturing and business and finance. These diplomas enable young people to get practical experience as well as continuing their learning in the classroom.

These students in Coventry, England, are studying for GCSE examinations. GCSE stands for General Certificate of Secondary Education. The exams are normally taken by students aged 15-16.

State and public schools

Ninety-three per cent of the students in the UK are educated at state schools. Some state schools are known as church schools. They were originally run by the church. Today they are run by local education authorities, though members of a church are usually given the choice to attend such schools before the rest of the community is offered places.

The other 7 per cent of students in the UK are educated in public schools, including well-known schools like Eton and Winchester College. Although called public schools, they are not paid for by the government. Instead, the family of the pupils who attend them usually pay between £10,000 and £20,000 per year directly to the school.

Universities

The UK has some of the world's oldest and best-known universities, such as Oxford, Cambridge and the University of Edinburgh. In Scotland, the government pays for students to attend university, while in Wales and Northern Ireland students can get grants to help them pay for their studies. In England, however, students must pay to attend university.

Oxford is the UK's oldest university. Parts of Christ Church College, Oxford, were used as a setting for the Harry Potter movies!

Employment and economy

There has been a big change in the type of work available in the UK over the last 20 years. In 1981 more than 30 per cent of jobs done by men were in traditional manufacturing industries like steel. Today less than 20 per cent of people work in manufacturing.

Biggest sectors

More than 30 million workers in the UK today are employed. Most of them work in what is known as the service sector. This sector includes industries such as education, financial services, tourism and health. Until recently, one in five people in the UK worked in financial and business services. Despite recent economic problems around the world, this is still the biggest sector of the UK economy.

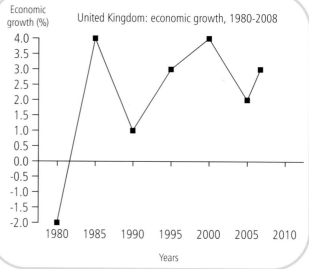

United Kingdom: economic growth, 1980-2008

Economic growth (%)

Years

⬇ Meetings, such as this one taking place at the Foundation for Art and Creative Technologies in Liverpool, are common for many UK business people.

Working families

The UK government tries to support working parents. Some working parents can get help by taking part of their salary in the form of childcare vouchers. The vouchers can be used to pay for childcare. Parents can also ask for flexible working to help them care for their family as well as going out to work. Still, it is difficult for many parents to juggle work and family life.

Unemployment

Unemployment, or the number of people out of work, has not been a problem in the UK since the 1980s, though this is changing. The UK unemployment rate has generally remained steady at about 6 per cent of the total workforce. Since March 2008, however, the number of people out of work has risen.

Women and work

Almost as many women as men work in the UK, but the jobs they do are often different. About 50 per cent of the jobs done by women are part-time, mainly in administrative or secretarial work. Men, on the other hand, are more likely to be managers or supervisors or perform a skilled trade like plumbing.

Men also earn more money than women. The 'pay gap' between what men and women earn is getting wider. Among full-time workers, men make about 17 per cent more money than women. This means that a full-time working woman earns about £400,000 less than a man during her lifetime. Most people blame the difference on the government, which has failed to make any rules about the pay gap.

DID YOU KNOW?
The NHS is the world's third-largest employer. Only Indian railways and the Chinese Army are bigger. Almost 1.3 million people work for the NHS, over 2 per cent of the UK population.

Facts at a glance

Contributions to GDP:
agriculture: 0.7%
industry: 21.8%
services: 77.5%
Labour force:
agriculture: 1.4%
industry: 18.2%
services: 80.4%
Female labour force:
45.4% of total
Unemployment rate: 7.8%

More than 65 per cent of UK mothers are employed, compared to 90 per cent of fathers.

Industry and trade

In recent years, service industries such as banking and finance have taken the place of manufacturing as the most important part of the UK economy. Today this industry is twice as large as manufacturing.

Changing times

Due to the onset of the economic downturn in 2008, the financial sector is undergoing many changes. One major change is the part-nationalisation of the banking system. This means that some banks are now owned or partially owned by the UK government. As a result, some banks that were once independently run are now partly run by the government.

▼ The City of London is one of the world's most important financial centres. Many of its most famous buildings were constructed in the 1980s and 1990s on land which was once home to dockland warehouses and factories.

An island-nation

As an island-nation, Great Britain has traditionally had a strong navy and a large fishing fleet. It also had large natural coal and mineral reserves, and coal mining in particular shaped the landscape of large parts of Yorkshire and South Wales.

In the 1970s the UK started to drill the natural oil reserves beneath the North Sea. For a few years the UK was self-sufficient in oil, but its oil and gas reserves are now falling. Recently the UK has been exploring alternative energy sources, including wind and wave power, as well as nuclear energy. There are now more than 200 wind farms in the UK and the government recently announced that more nuclear power stations would be built.

△ The UK government set a target for 10 per cent of the UK's energy to come from renewable sources like wind power.

Imports and exports

More goods and services are imported to the UK than exported. However, the petro chemical industry is the largest export earner, and British Petroleum (BP) is the UK's largest company. The UK also exports services such as banking and finance. Imports include manufactured goods such as cars as well as machinery and food.

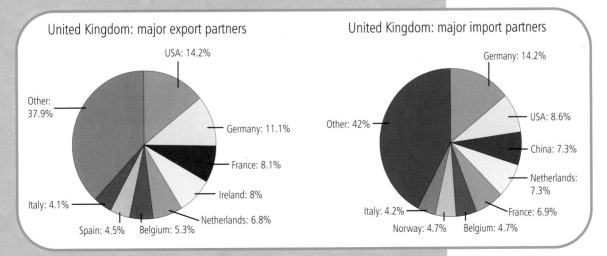

United Kingdom: major export partners

USA: 14.2%
Other: 37.9%
Germany: 11.1%
France: 8.1%
Ireland: 8%
Netherlands: 6.8%
Belgium: 5.3%
Spain: 4.5%
Italy: 4.1%

United Kingdom: major import partners

Germany: 14.2%
USA: 8.6%
China: 7.3%
Netherlands: 7.3%
France: 6.9%
Belgium: 4.7%
Norway: 4.7%
Italy: 4.2%
Other: 42%

Farming and food

More than three-quarters of the land in the UK is used for farming. Agriculture employs over half a million people and there are more than 300,000 farms in the UK. Each has an average of 57 hectares, meaning that farms in the UK are larger than the European average of about 20 hectares.

Modern agriculture

Farms vary widely across the UK. Highland areas of Scotland, for instance, and large parts of Wales are grazed by sheep. Dairy farming is common in the west of England, where lots of rain helps the grass that cows feed on to grow. Crops such as wheat, barley and vegetables are most common in the east of England.

Today's farms in the UK are highly efficient. They use special machinery to help them grow and harvest their crops. Less than 2 per cent of the UK workforce provides 60 per cent of the UK's food needs.

Facts at a glance

Farmland: 24% of total land area

Main agricultural exports: prepared food, beverages

Main agricultural imports: animal and vegetable materials, prepared food

Average daily calorie intake: 3,440 calories

▼ Farms in the UK often use specialised machinery to harvest crops.

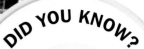

A changing diet

British meals have traditionally been based on meat or fish, with potatoes and other vegetables added. Although fishing in the UK has fallen in recent years, fish remains an important part of the British diet. Migration has also had an impact on what people in the UK eat. Both Chinese and Indian foods are popular in the UK diet.

Traditional to modern

Many UK meals have a strong regional identity. A 'ploughman's lunch' – made of cheese and bread with pickles – is based on traditional food eaten by agricultural workers in England. A Cornish pasty is a type of pie first made for Cornish tin miners. Haggis is a Scottish dish traditionally eaten on Burns Night. This event celebrates the birthday of Robert Burns, an eighteenth-century Scottish poet who was born on 25 January 1759.

Modern British food is a style of cuisine that takes traditional British recipes and combines them with recipes from other countries.

○ Some UK farmers sell their produce directly to customers at special farmers' markets like this one at Lewes in East Sussex. This saves transport costs as well as helping the environment.

▼ A traditional Scottish meal of haggis, *neeps* (swede) and *tatties* (mashed potatoes) is served on Burns Night.

Transport and communications

Most journeys in the UK are taken by car. In rural areas more than 50 per cent of families own two or more cars. This is because public transport is often poor in the countryside.

Rail transport

Travelling by rail in the UK can be expensive, although the number of people using trains has gone up since 1994. This is partly because the government is trying to increase the use of public transport in order to ease congestion on the roads.

Heavy road use

The distance travelled in an average year by cars and lorries on UK roads is more than 500 billion kilometres (310 billion miles). This can sometime lead to problems as many UK roads can't cope with so much traffic. Efforts to reduce this problem include the creation of a national network of cycle routes, which already covers more than 19,500 km (12,000 miles). All major employers are now required to draw up travel plans to encourage measures such as car-sharing to help ease traffic congestion.

Many cycle routes – like this one between Long Marston and Stratford-upon-Avon – follow the route of disused railway lines. The flat, wide track-bed makes for easy cycling.

DID YOU KNOW?
The UK's roads are some of the busiest in the world. On average, UK motorists together spend more than 114 million hours each year stuck in traffic jams!

In the air

In 2007, 241 million passengers used UK airports, and air travel – both in and out of the UK – is increasing. This has led to the rapid expansion of many UK airports. In 2008, London's biggest airport – Heathrow – added a fifth terminal. It also began construction of Heathrow East to replace Terminal 2. The government also approved plans to build a third runway in 2009. Many people are against this, however, arguing that more flights will increase the damage done to the environment by global warming, for example. In addition, people living near airports suffer from increased noise pollution.

Communications

The World Wide Web was invented by the English computer scientist Sir Tim Berners-Lee. Today more than 60 per cent of households in the UK have access to the World Wide Web. Most people use the Internet every day. Some regularly shop online. Most people in the UK have access to a mobile phone and almost 90 per cent of homes have a telephone.

⚫ Passengers can get on a train at the new Eurostar terminal at St Pancras station, London, and be in Paris in a little over two hours.

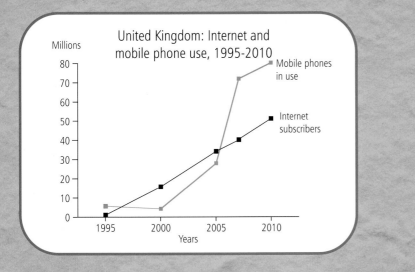

United Kingdom: Internet and mobile phone use, 1995-2010

Millions

Mobile phones in use

Internet subscribers

Years

Leisure and tourism

The most popular leisure activity of all in the UK is eating out. Walking or rambling, visiting friends and shopping are also common. At home, people in the UK watch an average of more than two hours of television each day.

Sports

Football is the most popular sport in the UK. More people become members of a football team than join any other type of club. Cricket is also very popular in England and Wales. Many people golf all around the UK, but especially in Scotland, where the game was invented.

There are many popular walking and hiking destinations in the UK, such as Crib Goch in Snowdonia, Wales.

Culture

The UK has a rich and varied cultural heritage, and the houses where famous poets, painters and playwrights lived are often popular with tourists. The famous playwright William Shakespeare was born in the UK in Stratford-upon-Avon. His plays are performed there throughout the year, as well as being studied by all UK schoolchildren. Shakespeare's birthplace is one of the most popular destinations for foreign tourists.

Going on holiday

Tourism provides jobs for more than 2 million people in the UK, or 7 per cent of the working population. The UK is a popular destination for foreign tourists. In 2007 more than 30 million people visited the UK, with the most popular destinations being London, Edinburgh and Bath.

Due to cheaper air-travel and higher earnings, people in the UK are now able to take more holidays themselves. The most popular foreign holiday destinations for UK residents are Spain and France. Greece is the third most popular destination for Britons, with the USA in fourth place.

🔺 The colourful Notting Hill Carnival is the second-largest street festival in the world. It is held every August in London and attracts millions of spectators.

🔻 Tourists stroll along the seafront in Llandudno, Wales's largest resort town.

DID YOU KNOW?
Foreign tourists spend more than £35 billion a year in the UK. That's enough to build the channel tunnel (which connects the UK with continental Europe) three times over!

Environment and wildlife

The UK is a relatively small, densely populated country. As a result the environment is under pressure from building, industrial activity and intensive farming. One of the challenges facing the UK in the twenty-first century is preserving the environment and protecting wildlife in the face of these pressures.

Protecting wildlife

There are more than 2,000 different animal species living in Britain. This makes the UK one of the most diverse wildlife habitats in the world. The UK provides breeding and winter feeding grounds for hundreds of migrant bird species. UK waters are home to 40 per cent of the European population of common seals. But some species are in decline, including the otter, dormouse, water vole and red squirrel. Attempts to preserve these species include protecting large areas of the countryside and encouraging wildlife-friendly farming.

◀ The red squirrel is under threat in the UK because of the loss of its long-term habitat and due to competition from grey squirrels. The number of red squirrels is now less than 200,000 in the UK, and continues to fall.

Facts at a glance

Proportion of area protected: 15.3%

Biodiversity (known species): 2,283

Threatened species: 33

28

Global Warming

The UK has experienced some unusual extremes of weather in recent years, ranging from drought conditions to widespread flooding. Many people believe these are a result of a worldwide rise in temperatures, called global warming. Parts of Scotland popular for winter skiing have suffered for several winters from a lack of snow.

Rubbish and recycling

The UK dumps more rubbish into landfill sites than any other EU country. People in the UK recycle just over 30 per cent of their household waste, but this is set to increase sharply. By 2020 the UK government has pledged that no more than 35 per cent of household waste will go to landfills. Local councils will face fines of £150 per tonne for any waste that exceeds this target.

The UK experienced severe floods in the summer of 2007. Here, children are playing in a flooded street in Yorkshire.

UK households create 35.1 million tonnes of waste every year. Of that, 9.4 million tonnes are recycled or composted.

Glossary

civil partnership legal relationship between two people, similar to marriage

climate normal weather conditions of an area

colony a country controlled by another country

culture way of life and traditions of a particular group of people

democracy form of government in which people vote for their leaders

diplomas higher education qualifications

economy way that trade and money are controlled by a country

empire countries ruled over by another nation

export good or service that is sold to another country

financial having to do with money or banking

GDP the total value of goods and services produced by a country

habitat the place, or type of place, where a plant or animal normally lives

Head of State the public leader of a country

Hindu someone who follows the beliefs of Hinduism, a religion originally from India

immigration movement of people to a foreign country to live

import good or service that is bought from another country

industry any activity that processes or manufactures raw materials into finished products

intensive farming method of farming used to produce the highest amount of crops possible

Jurassic a period of time long before humans

landscapes physical features (such as mountains, rivers and deserts) of a place

latitude how far north or south a place is from the equator

manufacturing making products, usually from raw materials

migration movement of people from one place to another

monarch the king, queen or emperor of a country

pension payments made to someone after they have stopped working for a living

petro-chemical a product made from oil; there are many different types of petrochemical products, from fuel for motor vehicles to plastics

political relating to the ideas of a group of people involved in government

premature something that happens earlier than it should

rural to do with the countryside or agriculture

service sector part of the economy that provides services such as banking, retail, education and health care

Sikh someone who follows the beliefs of Sikhism, a religion originally from India

temperate a mild climate that is neither extremely hot nor extremely cold

terminal the place where a particular journey finishes

unemployment being without paid work

urban to do with towns and town life

Victorian dating from the time of Queen Victoria

World Heritage Site a list of outstanding natural or cultural places in the world created by the United Nations Educational, Scientific and Cultural Organization (UNESCO) to help protect and preserve the sites

Topic web

**Use this topic web to explore UK themes
in different areas of your curriculum.**

History
Find out more about the British Empire. Find out which countries are now members of the Commonwealth, and when they became independent.

Geography
Parts of the UK are below sea-level and at risk of flooding. Use an atlas to find out where these places are. Then shade them in on a map of the UK.

Science
'Reduce – recycle – reuse' is the UK's motto as it tries to reduce harm to the environment. Make a list of things you could do to reduce energy consumption in your home.

Maths
World clocks are calculated from the Greenwich Meridian, which runs through London. Choose five world cities outside the UK and work out what the time will be when it is midday in the UK.

United Kingdom

English
William Shakespeare is one of the world's most famous writers. Find out about his life and work and write a short biography of him.

Citizenship
The UK is a member of the European Union. Find out more about the EU. How many countries are EU members? List some of the advantages of being in the EU.

Design and Technology
In traditional England and Scotland, a coat of arms was used to represent a person or a group of people. Research coats of arms and then design a coat of arms to represent yourself.

ICT
Imagine you are planning to visit a World Heritage Site in the UK. Use the Internet to decide where you want to go and what you want to see.

Further information and index

Further reading

UK (World in Focus), Alex Woolf (Wayland 2008)
Great Britain (Country Topics), Richard and Sheila Tames (Franklin Watts 2007)
Great Britain (Country Files), Clare Oliver (Franklin Watts 2006)
England, (Welcome to My Country), Maree Lister (Franklin Watts 2010)

Web

http://news.bbc.co.uk/1/hi/world/europe/country_profiles/1038758.stm
This is the BBC's country profile of the UK. You can find lots of background information and a timeline of major events in UK history.
http://www.visitbritain.co.uk/about-britain/
On this site you can see pictures of the UK, find out about some of the UK's top tourist destinations and find information on the British weather!

Index